MORE PRAISE FOR ILLUMINATE

"Kerrie O' Brien gifts us a pure poetry of the senses. Her world is rich with its startling and honest scrutiny of people and places, of states of mind and twilit in-betweens. The writing demonstrates a refreshing openness to language and feeling, and is as colourful as it is spare and understated. Her sense of the city is sublime, whether writing of Dublin or Paris, and her response to the iconic shapers of visual culture original. Through her eyes, the fragile world we inhabit is illuminated: raw, erotic, tender, but aflame with a poetically controlled feeling that ranges from lament to celebration. O' Brien's vision is beautiful and out of the ordinary, and this is one of the best collections I have read this year."

Mary O'Donnell

"Kerrie O' Brien's poems communicate in a kind spontaneous language that is pared down to the essentials in a way that truthfully reflects and illuminates her felt emotions and what she sees as the impermanence of things. They reveal a poet of marked sensibility and delicate cadences."

Gerard Smyth

salmonpoetry

Celebrating 35 Years
of Literary Publishing

ILLUMINATE

KERRIE O' BRIEN

Published in 2016 by
Salmon Poetry
Cliffs of Moher, County Clare, Ireland
Website: www.salmonpoetry.com
Email: info@salmonpoetry.com

ISBN 978-1-910669-47-1

COVER ARTWORK & FRONT COVER DESIGN: *Karen Comerford*

BACK COVER DESIGN & BOOK TYPESETTING: *Siobhán Hutson*

Printed in Ireland by Sprint Print

Salmon Poetry gratefully acknowledges the support of
The Arts Council / An Chomhairle Ealaoín

For the McCaffrey family

Acknowledgements

I wish to thank the Arts Council of Ireland for making this book possible.

Thank you to the following publications and programmes where some of this work has previously appeared: *The Irish Times, Hennessy New Irish Writing, The Literateur, Sunday Miscellany, Banshee, The Ofi Press, The Bohemyth, Wordlegs, HeadStuff, The Weary Blues, The Poetry Bus* and *ROPES 2016*.

Huge thanks to Mary O'Donnell, Theo Dorgan, Gerard Smyth, Nessa O'Mahony, Pat Cotter, Connie Roberts, Doireann Ní Ghríofa, Andrew McMillan and all the other writers who helped me with this manuscript.

Thank you to Liam Donnelly and all the staff of Hodges Figgis, Dubray Book and Books Upstairs.

Thank you to Jessie Lendennie and the amazing work of Siobhán Hutson from Salmon Poetry.

Thank you to Jack Harte, Caroline Williams, Sebastian Barry and Arthur Broomfield for their continuous support and encouragement. Finally thank you to my incredible family and Ian Kinane, Mary McAuley, Liv Monaghan, Natasha Mahon, Dave Flanagan, Caitriona Coakley, Jenny Murray, Sarah Noonan, JR Ryall, Jan Coll, Stephen James Smith, Dave Rudden, Sarah Griffin, Doireann Markham, Cathal Sherlock, Sara O'Loughlin, Caoimhe Hanley and my mother Mary McCaffrey. I couldn't have done this without any of you.

Contents

Soul clap its hands and sing, and louder sing

William Butler Yeats

ILLUMINATE

Morning Sun

The bed faced the window

So I would wake to brightness
Stretch in its warmth

And contemplate the rooftops
Of the city.

I felt like one of Hopper's
Solitary women
Rose pale, dappled gold

Made of light and shadow.

Miss you, try not to
Know you felt it

Same mind, blue threads
The red tether
The hunger.

Shiver in the memory
Then bathe

Gentle with my body

Watch the steam
Rise and swirl

And float
Swanlike
My heart softly
Expanding –

The room
Full of bright cloud.

Rothko

They found him
Hunched over a
White sink
All his beauty let out.

I think of him in his studio
East Hampton 1964
Wooden beams
Stained,
Concrete floor

Sitting in a dark green chair
Head tilted, cigarette in hand
Peering at his creation
Layers and pain
Towering before him
Lost to it,

One mere man
What he gave

I see him with wings

Immersed in his
Low lit hush
Portals expanding
Crimson lilac
Burnt orange, greys

Weighted hum
Solemn yet violent

Fire, heart
Bloodsweat
Spilling out

So close and strange
People weep

Sacred –

What we do to each other
And give
Without knowing.

Ashes

Is it her memory or mine?
Each bit so slow and vivid
I must have followed her
Through the house
Watching –

No need for talk
As she roused the days,
Opening slow and bleary

It was ritual, ceremonious
On her knees like a witch
Whispering to the ashes
Invoking
Fires, red flowers
From her sleeve

Her mouth a bellows
Coaxing blushes
From shy embers –
Grey birds fluttering
Allowing.

Some burn for centuries
In old houses
Ancient art passed
Down, murmuring
In the blood lines

Here now
Here with me.

Seine

It had usually been snowing
Courtyard veiled in a hush

The sky
White smoke
And sugar rose

The days could take you anywhere

I would wrap up my body
And follow the streets

The air pure
The relief of it

Walking in a state of grace –

I felt guided
I felt brave

The breath at my mouth
A cold sweetness

And finally –
The river

Grey jewel
In sun glimmer

Numb
Unmoving

But beneath it

A blue clamour
A blue star

Raw and flaming
Hooked to life

Pulsing fire
In all things.

Barrie Cooke

His electric elk

White mist,
And blood shadow

The kind that demands respect

To confuse a predator
A herd will scatter
To the four winds –

I knew every bit
Had stared for hours
At a book of his works

Always that one
Inexplicable draw

A symbol of stamina,
Agility, persistence

Privately kept
No chance of ever seeing it –
But here he was

Floating in the dark
Waiting for me in Paris

As if I was being protected
As if all moments

Happen at once.

Beckett

I go to visit him
Where he lies in Montparnasse

His portrait on my wall
Greets me sternly in the mornings

Chiseled and suspicious
But beautiful

Layered ochre white blue
One of the Le Brocquys.

On my way
A girl stops me for directions

Tells me she is Lebanese
And that her name is Maia

Goddess of earth and spring
And beginnings

Then offers me a Vogue cigarette
Thin, rose flavoured –

I take it as a sign that things
Will be alright

And that I should bring him flowers
An offering

Red flurry in pale light

Close by
I find Sontag and de Beauvoir

And it seems fitting
But get no sense of him –

Because really
On warm evenings
He is at home
Near Cooldrinagh

Still roaming the hills
With his father.

Core

You need to be very still
To hear the concert of your body

To think about what you contain

Salt and water
Know what it's doing
Renewing itself
Back to earth

It is a quiet thing
This is where our riches are

We are all red inside
Brimming with love

All fluid and quiet and fire.

Inherent

My great-grandmother had it
Though few will talk of it
How she lived on a hill
Closer to the heavens

Lighthouse

Where the cloud shadow
Would change the colour
Of the fields
Screaming yellow in July

They would come for
Miles to be healed
Wide holes in their flesh
A lifetime smoking pipes –

Drawn by a promise
Following the star
Of her bright elixir

Bird feather
Suspended
In glass

Something about this
Stirs memory
Trembles within me

The burning urge to cure.

Matisse

Had no time for twilight
When he could no longer walk
He used long bamboo
Painting up high
On his white walls

His last shapes
And cut-outs so simple
You'd think them
The marks of a child

So joyful, they move –

His blue acrobat
Leaps on my wall.

That yearning – still
That undying need
To create

As if one final work could
Sum it all up

Screaming look, *look*
I am done.

We are never done –
Nothing
Is ever done or over
No clean break

In love we are always endless –

My whole life
Fireflies
In circles.

I will always remember
That first sight

I couldn't keep my eyes off
I wanted to be close

And love

Fuelled through my body
Rose hot and lit me up –

I hope the last thought
I have of you
Is the same
As the first.

You Come To Me

Days after she has left
I remember it in a kind of
Bright fog
You so – raw

You'd seen me through it
A cafe overlooking Pompidou
Everything let out.

You looked young in the mornings
Because mornings are beginnings
Hot coffee in January light
Shivering – then you broke

After days of nothings
You were talking of God
And suddenly crying
Fiercely

Like you were raining.

I took your hands in mine
As I had taken my Grandfather's
When he thought the end was coming –

Only touch will do
In these moments
Each time the same prayer –

You mean so much to me.

They came then
Above and around us

Feathered lightness
White arcs
Swooping in from the river

Alive and immediate

Oh tell me
The dead don't speak
Don't love –
I tell you they do.

Musée de l'Orangerie

Quietest place
On earth

Where Nymphéas bloom
Dying of their love

Lily cloud willow sky

Rose fragments
In endless blue

In their light
You could be anything.

I sit while the world flickers
While the world screams

Liminal space

And beyond them

The Champs-Élysées
Fields of Elysium.

Is that what it's like

A circle
Oneness
Brief gap in the chaos

We dissolve
Soundless

And come out
The other side

Transformed,
Unafraid

And continue
Our infinite being.

Ephemeral

I saw white butterflies
Déjà vu that first morning after
Like we'd seen this all before

They say it's a sign
Of how you died
In a past life

On my left arm, near my heart
Like a scorch mark from a bullet
A sign you're not through with the pain
A reminder – I've lived – I've been

You noticed it and said
I have the same mark
It was there on your arm

Down near your hand
The same shape

And when we would sleep that way
They would touch – matching wounds
Whatever it was
It went through us both.

Hemingway

One of the days it was too cold
To do anything but sit
And read in Shakespeare & Co.

The air thick with spirit

Learning of his time in Paris
When he was my age
The fires, snow, hunger, love

He was talking of the winds
At the river
How they would cut you
In gusts by the bridges

Better to slowly climb
The back streets
Huddle low in the silence.

I knew where he meant
Felt it like a slap –

How could he be so close
And I not know it –

The worst time to search
Whiteout, blizzard sleet

I hadn't eaten
The hunger raw and persisting

But he led me
And right where he lived

A café

Rose star
In the wilderness
Warm jewel

Run by an American woman
Big hearted

Who took me in
And gave me a muffin
Flooded with raspberry –
Bloodsweet, glittering, hot.

It then came
A thudding chant –

Be still, still
In the howling.

Have faith
Just a little longer.

Notre Dame

Certain mornings
I would be the only one
To see the first streams of it

Tumbling through stained glass
Smattering everything
Red gold rose blue.
The beauty almost frightening.

Yves Klein would daub his women
Blue
And hurl them at the canvas.

Living brushes
Haphazard and outrageous –
Same effect.
Different every day
This glittering cave
Big beautiful lit up thing.

It knew and knew
Why I had come.

Falling like water
Blue gold rose red
My river walk,
My morning prayer.

I would step into it slow
Circling the altar
Gold cross flickering
In the centre
Anchored, rooted still.

As above, so below

Eyes closed
Filling my heart
With the warmth of it

Until my body was
Sunlight and roses
And the fear
Fell away in petals

Would you believe it
If I told you
Nothing felt separate.

Diane Arbus

Black and white drag queens
Meet your gaze
Staring from Metro posters

The last day of her retrospective

Waiting outside Jeu de Paume
Gold neon of the ferris wheel
Rippling in circles

Everything doubled
And gleaming in the rain

We had to dance to keep warm
But worth it

Stepping into her underworld
Her life –

Perhaps she saw too much.

One of them looked like us –
A teenage couple on Hudson Street

Embracing
Like they were the same being

Twin stars, luminous
Bound to each other

Odd and synchronistic
But things always were
With you

And I didn't know
That in a few months
I would be on that street

Eating Mexican food
On the hottest of days

The fresh chilli
Glittering my throat

That love could come back
And repeat itself
A thousandfold

That we would happen again.

Williamsburg

We ate avocado and chicken
After going to the Frick

Then found a café with a courtyard
And drank coffee in the haze

I waited outside
And looked all along the street
Where the heat rose off the pavement
And quivered

I felt I knew it, could feel

The blood of my ancestry
Its firewater

Their strength and metal
In the breeze
Everything glowing

Then you –
All worried
I didn't know you'd been looking

Twice now this had happened
And I could never understand it
Why would you be afraid of losing me?

Still troubled still the unease
So I took your hand

There was a park just on the corner
Prospect Park

I'm sure that's what it was called
I was so sure of everything then.

Guide

Your perfect white flat in East Berlin
Had a bathroom with no light
So you filled it with red candles
Like a chapel.

I had come shot,
Hoping the snow would deaden the spread of it

Sitting in the shower praying in the
Half-light with those red flames blazing
Like prophets like seers calling me back

In this city
Where everything is still missing
Where they're still rebuilding
You had found love

Like nothing before in your life
And it pulsed and shone all around you

Like tiny yellow birds
Singing me back to the root
Of the root I was learning

To see in the dark.

Phosphorescent

Heaven streams
Quivering jolts
In delirium heat

There were suddenly fireflies
At your shoulder

Burnt glimmers from ether

Gold fragments
Burning kites
Crackling the air

Bodies
Flickering in sync

All our stars out –

For so long I looked back
Blinkered, searching
Trying to make sense of it

The bittersweet impermanence
Of things

But nothing has been
Only being

Come, now, in
Further than before
Here where it's quiet
Breathe, breathe

Fall in the core of it

Go with me further now
Seek, seek
The gleam, the beat

Forget all that happened
Death has no place here

Oh see –

See them blaze forth
In their thousands.

John Moreland

I catch him by chance

Find him sitting
Spot lit, peering

A sage
Waiting in his cave

Only open
The odd afternoon now –

Dust motes dance
In the light.

Full of different times.

He poses with ease
The most photographed man
In Dublin

Eyes
Two blue stars

And hands
Delicate as butterflies.

He gives me a gift –
Rose buds
Pink and
Made of wafer

Ancient, sweet, precious

Reminding me
To teach only love

For that is all we are.

Austin Hugh

The only time I ever saw
Forked lightening
Blazing heart strings

London like a Pollock
Gold veined against blue

We were caught
On a walkway to the station
Made of glass and metal
Live wires –

I could have lost you

Then in the mess and clamour
Suddenly saw you
Like you were a young boy
Or a vision

Just like our grandmother
And the story –

How he appeared
At her weakest

At the end of the bed
Quietly standing
In a halo of bright flame

A fire angel

Gold spilling
From his heart

Helping her through
While she gave birth
To her last son

And the name carried on in him
And you.

There can be beauty in grief –

They come in when needed
Luminous in the whirl

Touching points

Continuations
The veil pulled back

As when two black holes collide
And time contracts
Then expands

As it witnesses the merging
Of the oldest stars.

Kings

They are the latest additions
Bundles of fun

While I sleep they are on trampolines
Or beaches

Photos come through in salt light
Hair flared bright by sun

Brandishing a freshly caught shark

Doing backflips in slow motion
Their true selves unfolding

My name spelled out in Lego
For my birthday

Or for the big matches
Robed emerald and gold

Two bright kings –
They are rooted in green.

4am my phone ignites
They are in a gallery in Melbourne

Blue-eyed like you
Gazing star struck

Beneath Ai Weiwei's
Forever Bicycles

Silver and whirling

More than a thousand –
Lit up in a violet hue

It is their first illumination.

And suddenly there is no distance.

The lineage
Like the old towers
Flaring the coast
One after one

The same blood
Flooded through us

Red threaded through gold

The honour.

Messenger

An old woman comes to collect
The book of poems she has ordered

I tell her I love Mary Oliver
Even though I haven't read much by her

She looks at me, smiles brightly
Beaming, giddy

Closing her eyes
She gives the words

Up on her toes, swaying

Singing the Red Bird to me
With such passion and urgency
She is declaring love

Her eyelids two quivering walnut shells
The years fall away

This young girl in trance
This red waterfall of joy

She looks at me again, at my eye
This seer, gracing my life
She has noticed the mark
Still there after months

And she says, were you angry?

I tell her I was, I was
And nearly fall into her arms.

Bud

I think you need to be empty
To fall in love

To have been pure in yourself
For long enough
To know who you are again.

There needs to have been a winter
Where you were bare
And elegant as an orchid

Moving towards the light but in no rush
Holding your grief well

Not waiting, expecting
But quietly knowing

There will be layers of new
Flowering softness

You will tremble with life

The buds will split open
Again and again.

Sculptor

Every moment or so
He wipes the ice
Which masks the stone
And tap, taps
Feeling for
The blood flow,
The pulse.

Slowly, the blows
Become soft.
Life awakens
Angels emerge
Beneath his hands.

What he creates
Will outlive him
Guarding the graves
Resurrecting dead
Memory.

At a dark hour
With one last touch
He will rise

White dust
Drifting
In his wake.

One Morning in Winter

Snow blooming at the window
White flowers of it
Bursting
Shivering wings

I am thinking of fireflies
And their bodies
All their lives
Making light

It is still, today
Rose flakes

Now birdsong
Oldest music
Pulse and fury

Tiny lungs
The sheer force
They dance and fall

I sing each one my prayer
Calling your spirit in

I need to make peace with
My heart, your heart

Firespark

Caught me at the start

I want to honour
What this was and
How close we got

I could say it all
A thousand different ways

My mantra
My cure
For every little thing –

I love you I am
Sorry please

Forgive me.

Sundays

Despite all the years that lie between us
We eat together each week

Eighty years of you, still strong

Clattering in the kitchen
Your ancient hands
Making everything look miniature.

Something powerful about your presence
An elegance
The whole family has some trace of it –
Striking.

You show your kindness by feeding me
Things you grow yourself

All the life you've had
Most of it I know nothing of

But I love you for it
Your pride and mystery

We sit, you quietly make tea

Pouring your heart out.

Turner

For one month only
To keep tradition

Every January

His bluegreen waters,
And apricot skies

A whole life chasing light

You wonder
Will they still do this
A thousand years from now

Or will everything eventually
Be forgotten.

And once –
A different presence in the room

A figure
Thin and distracting

Elegant as a heron
Lilac and grey

It was Le Brocquy

Standing otherworldly
In a Venice sunset

The last time he would see them
And I wonder did he sense it

Gazing
Transfixed by their glow

As when they first discovered
Fire gold fire oh

How they must have trembled
At the beauty.

Wish

I want to have the blessing
Of a deathbed

In a house that is a shrine
To all the favourite parts
Of my life

I want to thank the well-loved
Bark of my body
For all it has done.

I want my spirit to go out
Like a laughing child

Running through the fields

And all along the white
Sands of the sea

Ready for anything.

KERRIE O' BRIEN has been published in many journals and newspapers including *Cyphers, The Stinging Fly, The Irish Times, Banshee Lit, The Irish Examiner, Southword, Orbis* and *The Penny Dreadful*. In February 2012 she was the first poet to read as part of the New Writers Series in Shakespeare & Co., Paris. Her poem "Blossoms" was chosen as the winning entry in the Emerging Talent category of the 2011 iYeats Poetry Competition. Her flash fiction piece "That Night" won the RTE Arena Flash Fiction Competition 2012 and Culture Ireland sponsored her to read in Los Angeles in June of that year. She was one of the emerging writers chosen to read at the Cork Spring Poetry Festival 2013 as well as the Poetry Ireland Introductions Series, Listowel Writers' Week, Cuisle International Poetry Festival and at the London Irish Arts Centre. Her short fiction piece "Dole" features in the *New Planet Cabaret Anthology* published by New Island in association with RTE Arena. She was shortlisted for the Penny Dreadful Novella Prize 2015 and is currently working on her first novel. She has a BA in History of Art and Architecture from Trinity College Dublin. *Illuminate* is her debut collection of poetry and was made possible by a literature bursary from the Arts Council of Ireland.